Puke in the Potty

Brenda Watson

Illustrations by Sara Murlatt

ISBN: 979-8-90252-105-1   (Paperback)
ISBN: 979-8-90252-104-4   (eBook)

Printed in the United States of America

Acknowledgments

My ultimate thank you is to God for the many blessings and gifts he has bestowed upon me. To my family—Mom, Dad, Lori, Carrie, and Julie—thank you for your continued support, love, prayers, and encouragement throughout this entire journey. To my beautiful niece, Gabby, and all seven of my handsome nephews—Nathan, Kobe, Gage, Elijah, Kolton, Ezra, and Elliot—you all have a special place in my heart. Aunt B rocks!

KJ and Mommy, thank you for the inspiration to write this book. God truly works in mysterious ways.

It means the world to me to have all of you in my life while I chase my dreams. XOXO

Hello! My name is Kolton... I am not feeling very well. It's my belly that hurts, but I have a story to tell.

POP

I had a sensitive stomach as a child.

Too much junk food made my tummy go wild!

My tummy sent back whatever I ate.

Usually around a quarter to eight.

Then one night, when I got sick, my mommy said to me

"I am going to tell you a story today

That you will never forget what I am about to say.

I will tell a story that was told to me

Right around the age of three."

"Puke in the Potty," that's what my mama said

Especially not on your nice clean bed.

"Puke in the Potty, you big noodlehead"

That's what my twin brothers said.

"Yes! Puke in the Potty," said my older sister

Especially if your belly feels a twister.

"I agree, Puke in the Potty," my father said.

It's so much better than doing it in your bed!

No cleanup! No sheets changed!

No hair washing either!

Generation to generation will only make us wiser!

Shoot for any toilet, basket, or bin.

Just get something for it to go in!

"Puke in the Potty," that's what grown-ups do.

You should tell a friend to do it too!

Life is crazy, most everyone gets the flu.

If you tell the story, they will relate to you too!

So if I ever feel like I'm going to blow,

From the top of my head to my little pinky toe.

I will puke in the potty forever and ever,

But something tells me I will always remember.

Trust me, your parents will shout, "Hip Hip Hooray!"

and say, "Thank you for puking in the potty today!"